AF346260

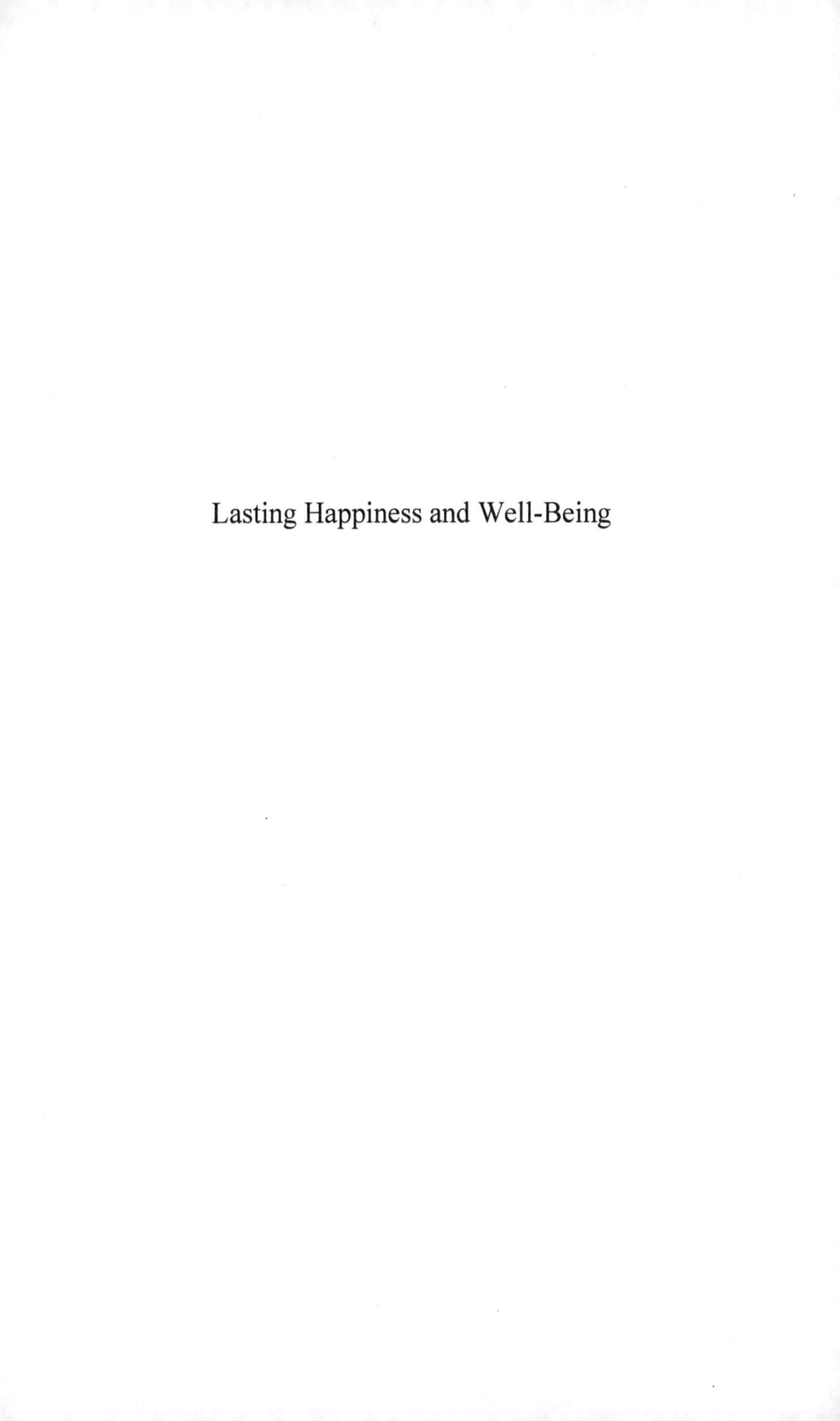

Lasting Happiness and Well-Being

Lasting Happiness and
Well-Being

Collection

by H. George Adams

"I have decided to be happy because it is good for my health."

- Voltaire

All men wish to live happily, said Seneca. Happiness, this mental state of satisfaction or lasting well-being, as we know it, is often difficult to acquire; especially when you live in a society where the sluggishness due to socio-economic problems seems to be contagious.

Under the title *The Secret of Abounding Happiness*[1], James Allen wrote :

Great is the thirst for happiness, and equally great is the lack of happiness. The majority of the poor long for riches, believing that their possession would bring them supreme and lasting happiness. Many who are rich, having gratified every desire and whim, suffer from ennui and repletion, and are farther from

---

[1] James Allen, in *From Poverty to Power; or, the Realization of Prosperity and Peace.*

the possession of happiness even than the very poor. If we reflect upon this state of things it will ultimately lead us to a knowledge of the all important truth that happiness is not derived from mere outward possessions, nor misery from the lack of them; for if this were so, we should find the poor always miserable, and the rich always happy, whereas the reverse is frequently the case. Some of the most wretched people whom I have known were those who were surrounded with riches and luxury, whilst some of the brightest and happiest people I have met were possessed of only the barest necessities of life. Many men who have accumulated riches have confessed that the selfish gratification which followed the acquisition of riches has robbed life of its sweetness, and that they were never so happy as when they were poor. What, then, is happiness, and how is it to be secured?

I used to wonder how do some people to be happy even in difficult socio-economic conditions? Have they found the path of happiness?

"I have decided to be happy because it is good for my health", said Voltaire, the French enlightenment philosopher. If happiness is good for our health why not develop the state of mind that allows us to reach it?

The purpose of this book is to help us to identify the road to happiness and develop the state of mind that leeds us on the path of well-being.

The decision for happiness and well-being

First of all, we must determine what makes us really happy, then look for how to reach it. Happiness seems difficult to achieve because there is no universal recipe to be happy. What some are looking for to be happy, others have already found it but they are still not happy. This is shown by the following quote : "I cried because I had no shoes until I met a man who had no feet".

This man, who could not afford shoes, had reason to complain and not be happy: he had to walk barefoot, everyday, everywhere, on burning ground, rocky and thorny, or in the cold. Those who have already walked barefoot in the warm sand, know how much the soles of the feet suffer from it, and they could confirm how nice it is to have shoes.

Yes, this man was right to think that he would be happier if he had shoes. However, he realized the privilege of having feet to walk when he met that disabled man for whom, having shoes was far from being his first concern. He would have been happy if only he could at least walk barefoot. Since that day he stopped complaining, and decided to appreciate his chance, this happiness of having feet to walk. He realized that others are more misfortuned.

Many things that we have, and to which we no longer pay attention, would make someone happy. Yes, the conditions of happiness are not the same for everyone.

We always think we could not be happy without certain conditions. Someone would say: I'd be so happy if I had a little more money. And he would remain in the unfortunate expectation of that day he would have enough money to be happy.

Another would say: I'd be happy if I could find the love of my life. And life would be morose to him if ever the dreamed love was found.

I would be so happy if I found work, would say another one. And during the period of unemployment he could not perceive all the other sources of happiness he has around him; his sadness would be so great.

We also hear others say: how to be happy with this gloomy weather? Ah, I would be happy if I could live in a sunnier region! And they are waiting for the good weather to be happy.

However, we have already seen richer people who are not really happy. They seem to have everything we need, but they didn't find happiness. Or people who live with the woman or the man of their life, who are not happy. They still miss something. Thus, the right question to ask oneself is this: have I really decided to be happy?

It is a wrong conception of happiness that prevents men from being able to reach it.[2] We are often persuaded, consciously or unconsciously, that happiness depends on what we have, who we are, or on satisfactory external factors. Studies have

---

[2] A. Libertad, in '*A la conquête du bonheur*'.

shown in recent years that those who are truly happy draw their joy and happiness from a state of mind that they have been able to cultivate over the years, transcending external factors and living conditions. It is the culmination of a construction that requires the will to achieve it.

Yes, happiness comes from other things than what we have or who we are.

To be happy, we have to consider this maxim of Confucius: "expect great things of yourself and demand little of others". Many seem unhappy because the actions of others do not meet their expectations. Although it is perfectly normal to be disappointed by the bad behavior of others, true happiness never escapes under the influence of annoyance. We can live relatively happily regardless of the conditions in which we are, said Emile Coue known for his concept of autosuggestion which is a force that can help us to live happily. If you want it, he said, you can do it. If some are happy or unhappy, it is that they imagine themselves to be so. It is possible for two persons in exactly the same circumstances to be, the one perfectly happy, the other absolutely wretched. It is what we discover throughout the history of these two women who raise their children alone, and were fired from their job. The first women we called here Francesca, said in tears "we have given all our life for this company and that's how we are thanked." And the days after were very hard for her. She is plunged into an inconsolable moroseness, with anger and resentment towards the employer. What ungrateful man! she said to herself unceasingly. Then, the anger turned into a shame. She felt devalued because she is unemployed; and could not stand the gaze of others who seemed to judge her. To this shame, added worries for the days to come. "And if I cannot find work, how are we going to live?... And the daily needs, the children, the house ..." Her worries grew. Misfortune has invaded her being, and she has even lost the radiance of her face; then, she lost sleep.

Her reaction and worries contrasted greatly with those of her former coworker that we called Michelle, who seemed to be leading her life as if nothing had happened, even if losing her job was not easy for her either. "I know I have to find another job, but in the meantime, I enjoy spending more time with my children. As long as we have food to eat, it is not the end of the world if I am fired". It may seem an exaggeration to say that she could remain happy in this uncomfortable situation, but it was obvious when you see her. Whatever one may say, she focused on the positive side of her situation, and did not let herself be overwhelmed by worries. But, let's ask ourselves whether worries and anger could help her to find job more easily, or better manage her situation. We can remember this question of the Lord about the worries: "Who among you by worrying, can add a single moment to your life?" In other words, who could really improve his situation by being overwhelmed by worries?

A happy state of mind, can take over the worries and annoyances. And this state of mind must be developed.

The following essay written by the American author Arthur Timothy. S.[3], deals with the story of an old man who managed the secret to be happy:

A boon of inestimable worth is a calm, thankful heart – a treasure that few, very few, possess. We once met an old man, whose face was a mixture of smiles and sunshine. Wherever he went, he succeeded in making everybody about him as pleasant as himself. Said we, one day, – for he was one of that delightful class whom everybody feels privileged to be related to, –"Uncle, uncle, how *is* it that you contrive to be so happy? Why is your face so cheerful, when so many thousands

---

[3] *How to be happy* by Arthur T.S.

are craped over with a most uncomfortable gloominess?"

"My dear young friend," he answered, with his placid smile, "I am even as others, afflicted with infirmities; I have had my share of sorrow--some would say more – but I have found out the secret of being happy, and it is this:

Forget self.

"Until you do that, you can lay but little claim to a cheerful spirit. 'Forget what manner of man you are,' and think more with, rejoice more for, your neighbours. If I am poor, let me look upon my richer friend, and in estimating his blessings, forget my privations.

"If my neighbour is building a house, let me watch with him its progress, and think, 'Well, what a comfortable place it will be, to be sure; how much he may enjoy it with his family.' Thus I have a double pleasure – that of delight in noting the structure as it expands into beauty, and making my neighbour's weal mine. If he has planted a fine garden, I feast my eyes on the flowers, smell their fragrance: could I do more if it was my own?

"Another has a family of fine children; they bless him and are blessed by him; mine are all gone before me; I have none that bear my name; shall I, therefore, envy my neighbour his lovely children? No; let me enjoy their innocent smiles with him; let me *forget myself* – my tears when they were put away in darkness; or if I weep, may it be for joy that God took them untainted to dwell with His holy angels forever.

"Believe an old man when he says there is great pleasure in living for others. The heart of the selfish man is like a city full of crooked lanes. If a generous thought from some glorious temple strays in there, wo to it – it is lost. It wanders about, and wanders about, until enveloped in darkness; as the mist of selfishness gathers around, it lies down upon some cold thought to die, and is shrouded in oblivion.

"So, if you would be happy, shun selfishness; do a kindly deed for this one, speak a kindly word for another. He who is constantly giving pleasure, is constantly receiving it. The little river gives to the great ocean, and the more it gives the faster it runs. Stop its flowing, and the hot sun would dry it up, till it would be but filthy mud, sending forth bad odours, and corrupting the fresh air of Heaven. Keep your heart constantly travelling on errands of mercy--it has feet that never tire, hands that cannot be overburdened, eyes that never sleep; freight its hands with blessings, direct its eyes--no matter how narrow your sphere--to the nearest object of suffering, and relieve it.

"I say, my dear young friend, take the word of an old man for it, who has tried every known panacea, and found all to fail, except this golden rule:

"Forget self, and keep the heart busy for others."

The selfishness (or egoism) never leads to happiness. Sometimes it is good to be selfish, can we hear as advice to be happy. What ignorance of human nature! Should fear of deception and ungrateful attitudes lead us to believe that selfishness would allow us to be happier? Whoever makes the choice to be happy must instead avoid the temptation to be selfish.

The egoist runs behind his own pleasure and never grasps happiness. And his destiny is despair and sadness, because he expects happiness as something due to him; and "makes of his own happiness the law of those around him" said the philosopher Emile-Auguste Chartier also known as Alain. What he doesn't know is that happiness is found in generosity, without calculation; he gives rather than he receives.

The following pages of this book are based on different essays and philosophical treatises that help us to develop our knowledge and reflection on this subject: what really makes us happy, how to find the road of well-being and to share it with those around us.

Happiness is a state that results from the agreement between man and the circumstances in which he lives.

How to achieve happiness[4]

> *It is necessary that man should desire; it is requisite that he should act; it is incumbent he should labour, in order that he may be happy.*

Happiness is a mode of existence of which man naturally wishes the duration, or in which he is willing to continue. It is measured by its duration, by its vivacity. The greatest happiness is that which has the longest continuance: transient happiness, or that which has only a short duration, is called *Pleasure*; the more lively it is, the more fugitive, because man's senses are only susceptible of a certain quantum of motion. When pleasure exceeds this given quantity, it is changed into *anguish*, or into

---

[4] Based on the work of Baron d'Holbach.

that painful mode of existence, of which he ardently desires the cessation: this is the reason why pleasure and pain frequently so closely approximate each other as scarcely to be discriminated. Immoderate pleasure is the forerunner of regret. It is succeeded by ennui, it is followed by weariness, it ends in disgust: transient happiness frequently converts itself into durable misfortune. According to these principles it will be seen that man, who in each moment of his duration seeks necessarily after happiness, ought, when he is reasonable, to manage, to husband, to regulate his pleasures; to refuse himself to all those of which the indulgence would be succeeded by regret; to avoid those which can convert themselves into pain; in order that he may procure for himself the most permanent felicity.

Happiness cannot be the same for all the beings of the human species; the same pleasures cannot equally affect men whose conformation is different, whose modification is diverse. This no doubt, is the true reason why the greater number of moral philosophers are so little in accord upon those objects in which they have made man's happiness consist, as well as on the means by which it may be obtained. Nevertheless, in general, happiness appears to be a state, whether momentary or durable, in which man readily acquiesces, because he finds it conformable to his being. This state results from the accord, springs out of the conformity, which is found between himself and those circumstances in which he has been placed by Nature; or, if it be preferred, *happiness is the co-ordination of man, with the causes that give him impulse.*

The ideas which man forms to himself of happiness depend not only on his temperament, on his individual conformation, but also upon the habits he has contracted. *Habit* is, in man, a mode of existence — of thinking — of acting, which his organs, as well interior as exterior, contract, by the frequent reiteration of the same motion; from whence results the faculty of performing these actions with promptitude, of executing them with facility.

If things be attentively considered, it will be found that almost the whole conduct of man—the entire system of his actions— his occupations—his connexions—his studies—his amusements—his manners—his customs—his very garments—even his aliments, are the effect of habit. He owes equally to habit, the facility with which he exercises his mental faculties of thought—of judgment—of wit—of reason—of taste, etc. It is to habit he owes the greater part of his inclinations—of his desires—of his opinions—of his prejudices—of the ideas, true or false, he forms to himself of his welfare. In short, it is to habit, consecrated by time, that he owes those errors into which everything strives to precipitate him; from which everything is calculated to prevent him emancipating himself. It is habit that attaches him either to virtue or to vice: experience proves this: observation teaches incontrovertibly that the first crime is always accompanied by more pangs of remorse than the second; this again, by more than the third; so on to those that follow. A first action is the commencement of a habit; those which succeed confirm it: by force of combatting the obstacles that prevent the commission of criminal actions, man arrives at the power of vanquishing them with ease; of conquering them with facility. Thus he frequently becomes wicked from habit.

Man is so much modified by habit, that it is frequently confounded with his nature: from hence results, as will presently be seen, those opinions or those ideas, which he has called *innate*: because he has been unwilling to recur back to the source from whence they sprung: which has, as it were, identified itself with his brain. However this may be, he adheres with great strength of attachment to all those things to which he is habituated; his mind experiences a sort of violence, an incommodious revulsion, a troublesome distaste, when it is endeavoured to make him change the course of his ideas: a fatal predilection frequently conducts him back to the old track in despite of reason.

It is by a pure mechanism that may be explained the phenomena of habit, as well physical as moral; the soul, notwithstanding its spirituality, is modified exactly in the same manner as the body. Habit, in man, causes the organs of voice to learn the mode of expressing quickly the ideas consigned to his brain, by means of certain motion, which, during his infancy, the tongue acquires the power of executing with facility: his tongue, once habituated to move itself in a certain manner, finds much trouble, has great pain, to move itself after another mode; the throat yields with difficulty to those inflections which are exacted by a language different from that to which he has, been accustomed. It is the same with regard to his ideas; his brain, his interior organ, his soul, inured to a given manner of modification, accustomed to attach certain ideas to certain objects, long used to form to itself a system connected with certain opinions, whether true or false, experiences a painful sensation, whenever he undertakes to give it a new impulse, or alter the direction of its habitual motion. It is nearly as difficult to make him change his opinions as his language.

Here, then, without doubt, is the cause of that almost invincible attachment which man displays to those customs—those prejudices—those institutions of which it is in vain that reason, experience, good sense prove to him the inutility, or even the danger. Habit opposes itself to the clearest, the most evident demonstrations; these can avail nothing against those passions, those vices, which time has rooted in him—against the most ridiculous systems—against the most absurd notions—against the most extravagant hypotheses—against the strangest customs: above all, when he has learned to attach to them the ideas of utility, of common interest, of the welfare of society. Such is the source of that obstinacy, of that stubbornness, which man evinces for his religion, for ancient usages, for unreasonable customs, for laws so little accordant with justice, for abuses, which so frequently make him suffer, for prejudices of which he sometimes acknowledges the absurdity, yet is unwilling to divest himself of them. Here is the reason why nations contemplate the most useful novelties as mischievous innovations—why they believe they would be lost, if they were to remedy those evils to which they have become habituated; which they have learned to consider as necessary to their repose; which they have been taught to consider dangerous to be cured.

Education is only the art of making man contract, in early life, that is to say, when his organs are extremely flexible, the habits, the opinions, the modes of existence, adopted by the society in which he is placed. The first moments of his infancy are employed in collecting experience; those who are charged with the care of rearing him, or who are entrusted to bring him up, teach him how to apply it: it is they who developed reason in him: the first impulse they give him commonly decides upon his condition, upon his passions, upon the ideas he forms to himself of happiness, upon the means he shall employ to procure it, upon his virtues, and upon his vices. Under the eyes of his masters, the infant acquires ideas: under their tuition he learns to associate them, —to think in a certain manner,—to judge well or ill. They point out to him various objects, which they accustom him either to love or to hate, to desire or to avoid, to esteem or to despise. It is thus opinions are transmitted from fathers, mothers, nurses, and masters, to man in his infantine state. It is thus, that his mind by degrees saturates itself with truth, or fills itself with error; after which he regulates his conduct, which renders him either happy or miserable, virtuous or vicious, estimable or hateful. It is thus he becomes either contented or discontented with his destiny, according to the objects towards which they have directed his passions—towards which they have bent the energies of his mind; that is to say, in which they have shewn him his interest, in which they have taught him to place his felicity: in consequence, he loves and searches after that which they have taught him to revere — that which they have made the object of his research; he has those tastes, those inclinations, those phantasms, which, during the whole course of his life, he is forward to indulge, which he is eager to satisfy, in proportion to the activity they have excited in him, and the capacity with which he has been provided by Nature.

Man's true Interest, or the Ideas he forms to himself of Happiness.

If man unceasingly seeks after his happiness, he can only approve of that which procures for him his object, or furnishes him the means by which it is to be obtained.

What has been already said will serve in fixing our ideas upon what constitutes this happiness: it has been already shewn that it is only continued pleasure: but in order that an object may please, it is necessary that the impressions it makes, the perceptions it gives, the ideas which it leaves, in short, that the motion it excites in man should be analogous to his organization; conformable to his temperament; assimilated to his individual nature:—modified as it is by habit, determined as it is by an infinity of circumstances, it is necessary that the action of the object by which he is moved, or of which the idea remains with him, far from enfeebling him, far from annihilating his feelings, should tend to strengthen him; it is necessary, that without fatiguing his mind, exhausting his faculties, or deranging his organs, this object should impart to his machine that degree of activity for which it continually has occasion. What is the object that unites all these qualities? Where is the man whose organs are susceptible of continual agitation without being fatigued; without experiencing a painful sensation;

without sinking? Man is always willing to be warned of his existence in the most lively manner, as long as he can be so without pain. What do I say? He consents frequently to suffer, rather than not feel. He accustoms himself to a thousand things which at first must have affected him in a disagreeable manner; but which frequently end either by converting themselves into wants, or by no longer affecting him any way: of this truth tobacco, coffee, and above all brandy furnish examples: this is the reason he runs to see tragedies; that he witnesses the execution of criminals. In short, the desire of feeling, of being powerfully moved, appears to be the principle of curiosity; of that avidity with which man seizes on the marvellous; of that earnestness with which he clings to the supernatural; of the disposition he evinces for the incomprehensible. Where, indeed, can he always find objects in nature capable of continually supplying the stimulus requisite to keep him in activity, that shall be ever proportioned to the state of his own organization; which his extreme mobility renders subject to perpetual variation? The most lively pleasures are always the least durable, seeing they are those which exhaust him most.

That man should be uninterruptedly happy, it would be requisite that his powers were infinite; it would require that to his mobility he joined a vigor, attached a solidity, which nothing could change; or else it is necessary that the objects from which he receives impulse, should either acquire or lose properties, according to the different states through which his machine is successively obliged to pass; it would need that the essences of beings should be changed in the same proportion as his dispositions; should be submitted to the continual influence of a thousand causes, which modify him without his knowledge, and in despite of himself. If, at each moment, his machine undergoes changes more or less marked, which are ascribable to the different degrees of elasticity, of density, of serenity of the atmosphere; to the portion of igneous fluid circulating through his blood; to the harmony of his organs; to the order that exists between the various parts of his body; if, at every period of his existence, his nerves have not the same tensions, his fibres the same elasticity, his mind the same activity, his imagination the same ardour, &c. it is evident that the same causes in preserving to him only the same qualities, cannot always affect him in the same manner. Here is the reason why those objects that please him in one season displease him in another: these objects have not themselves sensibly changed; but his organs, his dispositions, his ideas, his mode of seeing, his manner of feeling, have changed:—such is the source of man's inconstancy.

If the same objects are not constantly in that state competent to form the happiness of the same individual, it is easy to perceive that they are yet less in a capacity to please all men; or that the same happiness cannot be suitable to all. Beings already various by their temperament, unlike in their faculties, diversified in their organization, different in their imagination, dissimilar in their ideas, of distinct opinions, of contrary habits, which an infinity of circumstances, whether physical or moral, have variously modified, must necessarily form very different notions of happiness. Those of a miser cannot be the same as those of a prodigal; those of a voluptuary, the same as those of one who is phlegmatic; those of an intemperate, the same as those of a rational man, who husbands his health. The happiness of each, is in consequence composed of his natural organization, and of those circumstances, of those habits, of those ideas, whether true or false, that have modified him: this organization and these circumstances, never being the same in any two men, it follows, that what is the object of one man's views, must be indifferent, or even displeasing to another; thus, as we have before said, no one can be capable of judging of that which may contribute to the felicity of his fellow man.

Interest is the object to which each individual according to his temperament and his own peculiar ideas, attaches his welfare; from which it will be perceived that this interest is never more than that which each contemplates as necessary to his happiness. It must, therefore, be concluded, that no man is totally without interest. That of the miser to amass wealth; that of the prodigal to dissipate it: the interest of the ambitious is to obtain power; that of the modest philosopher to enjoy tranquillity; the interest of the debauchee is to give himself up, without reserve, to all sorts of pleasure; that of the prudent man, to abstain from those which may injure him: the interest of the wicked is to gratify his passions at any price: that of the virtuous to merit by his conduct the love, to elicit by his actions the approbation of others; to do nothing that can degrade himself in his own eyes.

Thus, when it is said that *interest is the only motive of human actions;* it is meant to indicate that each man labours after his own manner, to his own peculiar happiness; that he places it in some object either visible or concealed; either real or imaginary; that the whole system of his conduct is directed to its attainment. This granted, no man can be called disinterested; this appellation is only applied to those of whose motives we are ignorant; or whose interest we approve. Thus the man who finds a greater pleasure in assisting his friends in misfortune than preserving in his coffers useless treasure, is called generous, faithful, and disinterested; in like manner all men are denominated disinterested, who feel their glory far more precious than their fortune. In short, all men are designated disinterested who place their happiness in making sacrifices which man considers costly, because he does not attach the same value to the object for which the sacrifice is made.

Man frequently judges very erroneously of the interest of others, either because the motives that animate them are too complicated for him to unravel; or because to be enabled to judge of them fairly, it is needful to have the same eyes, the same organs the same passions, the same opinions: nevertheless, obliged to form his judgment of the actions of mankind, by their effect on himself, he approves the interest that actuates them whenever the result is advantageous for his species: thus, he admires valour, generosity, the love of liberty, great talents, virtue, &c. he then only approves of the objects in which the beings he applauds have placed their happiness; he approves these dispositions even when he is not in a capacity to feel their effects; but in this judgment he is not himself disinterested; experience, reflection, habit, reason, have given him a taste for morals, and he finds as much pleasure in being witness to a great and generous action, as the man of *virtu* finds in the sight of a fine picture of which he is not the proprietor. He who has formed to himself a habit of practising virtue, is a man who has unceasingly before his eyes the interest that he has in meriting the affection, in deserving the esteem, in securing the assistance of others, as well as to love and esteem himself: impressed with these ideas which have become habitual to him, he abstains even from concealed crimes, since these would degrade him in his own eyes: he resembles a man who having from his infancy contracted the habit of cleanliness, would be painfully affected at seeing himself dirty, even when no one should witness it. The honest man is he to whom truth has shewn his interest or his happiness in a mode of acting that others are obliged to love, are under the necessity to approve for their own peculiar interest.

These principles, duly developed, are the true basis of morals; nothing is more chimerical than those which are founded upon imaginary motives placed out of nature; or upon innate sentiments; which some speculators have regarded as anterior to man's experience; as wholly independent of those advantages which result to him from its use: it is the essence of man to love himself; to tend to his own conservation; to seek to render his existence happy: thus interest, or the desire of happiness, is the only real motive of all his actions; this interest depends upon his natural organization, rests itself upon his wants, is bottomed upon his acquired ideas, springs from the habits he has contracted: he is without doubt in error, when either a vitiated organization or false opinions shew him his welfare in objects either useless or injurious to himself, as well as to others; he marches steadily in the paths of virtue when true ideas have made him rest his happiness on a conduct useful to his species; in that which is approved by others; which renders him an interesting object to his associates. *Morals* would be a vain science if it did not incontestably prove to man that *his interest consists in being virtuous.* Obligation of whatever kind, can only be founded upon the probability or the certitude of either obtaining a good or avoiding an evil.

Indeed, in no one instant of his duration, can a sensible, an intelligent being, either lose sight of his own preservation or forget his own welfare; he owes happiness to himself; but experience quickly proves to him, that bereaved of assistance, quite alone, left entirely to himself, he cannot procure all those objects which are requisite to his felicity: he lives with sensible, with intelligent beings, occupied like himself with their own peculiar happiness; but capable of assisting him, in obtaining those objects he most desires; he discovers that these beings will not be favorable to his views, but when they find their interest involved; from which he concludes, that his own happiness demands, that his own wants render it necessary he should conduct himself at all times in a manner suitable to conciliate the attachment, to obtain the approbation, to elicit the esteem, to secure the assistance of those beings who are most capacitated to further his designs. He perceives, that it is man who is most necessary to the welfare of man: that to induce him to join in his interests, he ought to make him find real advantages in recording his projects: but to procure real advantages to the beings of the human species, is to have virtue; the reasonable man, therefore, is obliged to feel that it is his interest to be virtuous. *Virtue is only the art of rendering himself happy, by the felicity of others*. The virtuous man is he who communicates happiness to those beings who are capable of rendering his own condition happy; who are necessary to his conservation; who have the ability to procure him a felicitous existence.

Such, then, is the true foundation of all morals; merit and virtue are founded upon the nature of man; have their dependence upon his wants. It is virtue alone that can render him truly happy: without virtue society can neither be useful nor indeed subsist; it can only have real utility when it assembles beings animated with the desire of pleasing each other, and disposed to labour to their reciprocal advantage: there exists no comfort in those families whose members are not in the happy disposition to lend each other mutual succours; who have not a reciprocity of feeling that stimulates them to assist one another; that induces them to cling to each other, to support the sorrows of life; to unite their efforts, to put away those evils to which nature has subjected them; the conjugal bonds, are sweet only in proportion as they identify the interest of two beings, united by the want of legitimate pleasure; from whence results the maintenance of political society, and the means of furnishing it with citizens. Friendship has charms only when it more particularly associates two virtuous beings; that is to say, animated with the sincere desire of conspiring to their reciprocal happiness. In short, it is only by displaying virtue, that man can merit the benevolence, can win the confidence, can gain the esteem, of all those with whom he has relation; in a word, no man can be independently happy.

Indeed, the happiness of each human individual depends on those sentiments to which he gives birth, on those feelings which he nourishes in the beings amongst whom his destiny has placed him; grandeur may dazzle them; power may wrest from them an involuntary homage; force may compel an unwilling obedience; opulence may seduce mean, may attract venal souls; but it is humanity, it is benevolence, it is compassion, it is equity, that unassisted by these, can without efforts obtain for him, from those by whom he is surrounded, those delicious sentiments of attachments, those soothing feelings of tenderness, those sweet ideas of esteem, of which all reasonable men feel the necessity. To be virtuous then, is to place his interest in that which accords with the interest of others; it is to enjoy those benefits, to partake of that pleasure which he himself diffuses over his fellows. He whom, his nature, his education, his reflections, his habits, have rendered susceptible of these dispositions, and to whom his circumstances have given him the faculty of gratifying them, becomes an interesting object to all those who approach him: he enjoys every instant, he reads with satisfaction the contentment, he contemplates with pleasure the joy which he has diffused over all countenances: his wife, his children, his friends, his servants greet him with gay, serene faces, indicative of that content, harbingers of that peace, which he recognizes for his own work: everything that environs him is ready to partake his pleasures; to share his pains; cherished, respected, looked up to by others, everything conducts him to agreeable reflections; he knows the rights he has acquired over their hearts; he applauds himself for being the source of a felicity that captivates all the world; his own condition, his sentiments of self-love, become an hundred times more delicious when he sees them participated by all those with whom his destiny has connected him. The habit of virtue creates for him no wants but those which virtue itself suffices to satisfy; it is thus that *virtue is always its own peculiar reward*, that it remunerates itself with all the advantages which it incessantly procures for others.

It will be said, and perhaps even proved, that under the present constitution of things, virtue far from procuring the welfare of those who practice it frequently plunges man into misfortune; often places continual obstacles to his felicity; that almost every where it is without recompense. What do I say? A thousand examples could be adduced as evidence, that in almost every country it is hated, persecuted, obliged to lament the ingratitude of human nature. I reply with avowing, that by a necessary consequence of the errors of his race, virtue rarely conducts man to those objects in which the uninformed make their happiness consist. The greater number of societies, too frequently ruled by those whose ignorance makes them abuse their power,—whose prejudices render them enemies of virtue,—who flattered by sycophants, secure in the impunity their actions enjoy, commonly lavish their esteem, bestow their kindness, on none but the most unworthy objects; reward only the most frivolous, recompense none but the most prejudicial qualities; and hardly ever accord that justice to merit which is unquestionably its due. But the truly honest man, is neither ambitious of remuneration, nor sedulous of the suffrages of a society thus badly constituted: contented with domestic happiness, he seeks not to augment relations, which would do no more than increase his danger; he knows that a vitiated community is a whirlwind, with which an honest man cannot co-order himself: he therefore steps aside; quits the beaten path, by continuing in which he would infallibly be crushed. He does all the good of which he is capable in his sphere; he leaves the road free to the wicked, who are willing to wade through its mire; he laments the heavy strokes they inflict on themselves; he applauds mediocrity that affords him security: he pities those nations made miserable by their errors,—rendered unhappy by those passions which are the fatal but necessary consequence; he sees they contain nothing but wretched citizens, who far from cultivating their true interest, far from labouring to their mutual felicity, far from feeling the real value of virtue, unconscious how dear it ought to be to them, do nothing but either openly attack, or secretly injure it; in short, who detests a quality which would restrain their disorderly propensities.

In saying that virtue is its own peculiar reward, it is simply meant to announce, that in a society whose views were guided by truth, trained by experience, conducted by reason, each individual would be acquainted with his real interests; would understand the true end of association; would have sound motives to perform his duties; find real advantages in fulfilling them; in fact, it would be convinced, that to render himself solidly happy, he should occupy his actions with the welfare of his fellows; by their utility merit their esteem, elicit their kindness, and secure their assistance. In a well-constituted society, the government, the laws, education, example, would all conspire to prove to the citizen, that the nation of which he forms a part, is a whole that cannot be happy, that cannot subsist without virtue; experience would, at each step, convince him that the welfare of its parts can only result from that of the whole body corporate; justice would make him feel, that no society, can be advantageous to its members, where the volition of wills in those who act, is not so conformable to the interests of the whole, as to produce an advantageous re-action.

But, alas! by the confusion which the errors of man have carried into his ideas: virtue disgraced, banished, and persecuted, finds not one of those advantages it has a right to expect: man is indeed shewn those rewards for it in a future life, of which he is almost always deprived in his actual existence. It is thought necessary to deceive, considered proper to seduce, right to intimidate him, in order to induce him to follow that virtue which everything renders incommodious to him; he is fed with distant hopes, in order to solicit him to practice virtue, while contemplation of the world makes it hateful to him; he is alarmed by remote terrors, to deter him from committing evil, which his associates paint as amiable; which all conspires to render necessary. It is thus that politics, thus that superstition, by the formation of chimeras, by the creation of fictitious interests pretend to supply those true, those real motives which nature furnishes,—which experience would point out,—which an enlightened government should hold forth,— which the law ought to enforce,—which instruction should sanction,— which example should encourage,-which rational opinions would render pleasant. Man, blinded by his passions, not less dangerous than necessary, led away by precedent, authorised by custom, enslaved by habit, pays no attention to these uncertain promises, is regardless of the menaces held out; the actual interests of his immediate pleasures, the force of his passions, the inveteracy of his habits, always rise superior to the distant interests pointed out in his future welfare, or the remote evils with which he is threatened; which always appear doubtful, whenever he compares them with present advantages.

Thus *superstition, far from making man virtuous by principle, does nothing more than impose upon him a yoke as severe as it is useless*; it is borne by none but enthusiasts, or by the pusillanimous;

who, without becoming better, tremblingly champ the feeble bit put into their mouth; who are either rendered unhappy by their opinions, or dangerous by their tenets; indeed, experience, that faithful monitor, incontestibly proves, that superstition is a dyke inadequate to resist the torrent of corruption, to which so many accumulated causes give an irresistible force: nay more, does not this superstition itself augment the public disorder, by the dangerous passions which it lets loose, by the conduct which it sanctions, by the actions which it consecrates? Virtue, in almost every climate, is confined to some few rational souls, who have sufficient strength of mind to resist the stream of prejudice; who are contented by remunerating themselves with the benefits they diffuse over society: whose temperate dispositions are gratified with the suffrages of a small number of virtuous approvers; in short, who are detached from those frivolous advantages which the injustice of society but too commonly accords only to baseness, which it rarely bestows, except to intrigue, with which in general it rewards nothing but crime.

In despite of the injustice that reigns in the world, there are, however, some virtuous men in the bosom even of the most degenerate nations; notwithstanding the general depravity, there are some benevolent beings, still enamoured of virtue; who are fully acquainted with its true value; who are sufficiently enlightened to know that it exacts homage even from its enemies; who to use the language of Ecclesiastes, "rejoice in their own works;" who are, at least, happy in possessing contented minds, who are satisfied with concealed pleasures, those internal recompenses of which no earthly power is competent to deprive them. The honest man acquires a right to the esteem, has a just claim to the veneration, wins the confidence, gains the love, even of those whose conduct is exposed by a contrast with his own. In short, vice is obliged to cede to virtue; of which it blushingly, though unwillingly, acknowledges the superiority. Independent of this ascendancy so gentle, of this superiority so grand, of this pre-eminence so infallible, when even the whole universe should be unjust to him, when even every tongue should cover him with venom, when even every arm should menace him with hostility, there yet remains to the honest man the sublime advantage of loving his own conduct; the ineffable pleasure of esteeming himself; the unalloyed gratification of diving with satisfaction into the recesses of his own heart; the tranquil delight of contemplating his own actions with that delicious complacency that others ought to do, if they were not hood-winked, No power is adequate to ravish from him the merited esteem of himself; no authority is sufficiently potent to give it to him when he deserves it not; the mightiest monarch cannot lend stability to this esteem, when it is not well founded; it is then a ridiculous sentiment: it ought to be considered, it really is *"vanity and vexation of spirit,"* it is not wisdom, but folly in the extreme; it ought to be censured when it displays itself in a mode that is mortifying to its neighbour, in a manner that is troublesome to others; it is then called arrogance; it is called vanity; but when it cannot be condemned, when it is known for legitimate when it is discovered to have a solid foundation, when it bottoms itself upon talents, when it rises upon great actions that are useful to the community, when it erects its edifice upon virtue; even though society should not set these merits at their just price, it is noble pride, elevation of mind, and grandeur of soul.

Of what consequence then, is it to listen to those superstitious beings, those enemies to man's happiness, who have been desirous of destroying it, even in the inmost recesses of his heart; who have prescribed to him hatred of his follower; who have filled him with contempt for himself; who pretend to wrest from the honest man that self-respect which is frequently the only reward that remains to virtue, in a perverse world. To annihilate in him this sentiment, so full in justice, this love of himself, is to break the most powerful spring, to weaken the most efficacious stimulus, that urges him to act right; that spurs him on to do good to his fellow mortals. What motive, indeed, except it be this, remains for him in the greater part of human societies? Is not virtue discouraged? Is not honesty contemned? Is not audacious crime encouraged? Is not subtle intrigue eulogized? Is not cunning vice rewarded? Is not love of the public weal taxed as folly; exactitude in fulfilling duties looked upon as a bubble? Is not compassion laughed to scorn? Are not traitors distinguished by public honors? Is not negligence of morals applauded,—

sensibility derided,—tenderness scoffed,—conjugal fidelity jeered,—sincerity despised,—enviolable friendship treated with ridicule: while seduction, adultery, hard- heartedness, punic faith, avarice, and fraud, stalk forth unabashed, decked in gorgeous array, lauded by the world? Man must have motives for action: he neither acts well nor ill, but with a view to his own happiness: that which he judges will conduce to this *"consummation so devoutly to be wished,"* he thinks his interest; he does nothing gratuitously; when reward for useful actions is withheld from him, he is reduced either to become as abandoned as others, or else to remunerate himself with his own applause.

This granted; the honest man can never be completely unhappy; he can never be entirely deprived of the recompense which is his due; virtue is competent to repay him for all the benefits he may bestow on others; can amply make up to him all the happiness denied him by public opinion; *but nothing can compensate to him the want of virtue.* It does not follow that the honest man will be exempted from afflictions: like, the wicked, he is subject to physical evils; he may pine in indigence; he may be deprived of friendship; he may be worn down with disease; he may frequently be the subject of calumny; he may be the victim to injustice; he may be treated with ingratitude; he may be exposed to hatred; but in the midst of all his misfortunes, in the very bosom of his sorrows, in the extremity of his vexation, he finds support in himself; he is contented with his own conduct; he respects himself;

he feels his own dignity; he knows the equity of his rights; he consoles himself with the confidence inspired by the justness of his cause; he cheers himself amidst the most sullen circumstances. These supports are not calculated for the wicked; they avail him nothing: equally liable with the honest man to infirmities, equally submitted to the caprices of his destiny, equally the sport of a fluctuating world, he finds the recesses of his own heart filled with dreadful alarms; diseased with care; cankered with solitude; corroded with regret; gnawed by remorse; he dies within himself; his conscience sustains him not but loads him with reproach; his mind, overwhelmed, sinks beneath its own turpitude; his reflection is the bitter dregs of hemlock; maddening anguish holds him to the mirror that shews him his own deformity; that recalls unhallowed deeds; gloomy thoughts rush on his too faithful memory; despondence benumbs him; his body, simultaneously assailed on all sides, bends under the storm of—his own unruly passions; at last despair grapples him to her filthy bosom, he flies from himself. The honest man is not an insensible Stoic; virtue does not procure impassibility; honesty gives no exemption from misfortune, but it enables him to bear cheerly up against it; to cast off despair, to keep his own company: if he is infirm, if he is worn with disease, he has less to complain of than the vicious being who is oppressed with sickness, who is enfeebled by years; if he is indigent, he is less unhappy in his poverty; if he is in disgrace, he can endure it with fortitude, he is not overwhelmed by its pressure, like the wretched slave to crime.

Thus the happiness of each individual depends on the cultivation of his temperament; nature makes both the happy and the unhappy; it is culture that gives value to the soil nature has formed; it is instruction that makes the fruit it produces palatable; It is reflection that makes it useful. For man to be happily born, is to have received from nature a sound body, organs that act with precision—a just mind, a heart whose passions are analogous, whose desires are conformable to the circumstances in which his destiny has placed him: nature, then, has done everything for him, when she has joined to these faculties the quantum of vigour, the portion of energy, sufficient to enable him to obtain those Proper things, which his station, his mode of thinking, his temperament, have rendered desirable. Nature has made him a fatal present, when she has filled his sanguinary vessels with an over-heated fluid; when she has given him an imagination too active; when she has infused into him desires too impetuous; when he has a hankering after objects either impossible or improper to be obtained under his circumstances; or which at least he cannot procure without those incredible efforts, that either place his own welfare in danger or disturb the repose of society. The most happy man, is commonly he who possesses a peaceful soul; who only desires those things which he can procure by labour, suitable to maintain his activity; which he can obtain without causing those shocks, that are either too violent for society, or troublesome to his associates. A philosopher whose wants are easily satisfied, who is a stranger, to ambition, who is contented with the limited circle of a small number of friends, is, without doubt a being much more happily constituted than an ambitious conqueror, whose greedy imagination is reduced to despair by having only one world to ravage. He who is happily born, or whom nature has rendered susceptible of being conveniently modified, is not a being injurious to society: it is generally disturbed by men who are unhappily born, whose organization renders them turbulent; who are discontented with their destiny; who are inebriated with their own licentious passions; who are infatuated with their own vile schemes; who are smitten with difficult enterprises; who set the world in combustion, to gather imaginary benefits in order to attain which they must inflict he heaviest curses on mankind, but in which they make their own happiness consist.

An Alexander requires the destruction of empires, nations to be deluged with blood, cities to be laid in ashes, its inhabitants to be exterminated, to content that passion for glory, of which he has formed to himself a false idea; but which his too ardent imagination, his too vehement mind anxiously thirsts after: for a Diogenes there needs only a tub with the liberty of appearing whimsical; a Socrates wants nothing but the pleasure of forming disciples to virtue.

Man by his organization is a being to whom motion is always necessary; he must therefore always desire it: this is the reason why too much facility In procuring the objects of his search, renders them quickly insipid. To feel happiness, it is necessary to make efforts to obtain it; to find charms in its enjoyment, it is necessary that the desire should be whetted by obstacles; he is presently disgusted with those benefits which have cost him but little pains. The expectation of happiness, the labour requisite to procure it, the varied prospects it holds forth, the multiplied pictures which his imagination forms to him, supply his brain with that motion for which it has occasion; this gives impulse to his organs, puts his whole machine into activity, exercises his faculties, sets all his springs in play, in a word, puts him into that agreeable activity, for the want of which the enjoyment of happiness itself cannot compensate him. Action is the true element of the human mind; as soon as it ceases to act, it falls into disgust, sinks into lassitude. His soul has the same occasion for ideas, his stomach has for aliment.

Thus the impulse given him by desire, is itself a great benefit; it is to the mind what exercise is to the body; without it he would not derive any pleasure in the aliments presented to him; it is thirst that renders the pleasure of drinking so agreeable; life is a perpetual circle of regenerated desires and wants satisfied: repose is only a pleasure to him who labours; it is a source of weariness, the cause of sorrow, the spring of vice to him who has nothing to do. To enjoy without interruption is not to enjoy any thing: the man who has nothing to desire is certainly more unhappy than he who suffers.

The happiness of man will never be more than the result of the harmony that subsists between his desires and his circumstances.

These reflections, grounded upon experience, drawn from the fountain of truth, ought to prove to man, that good as well as evil depends on the essence of things. Happiness to be felt cannot be continued. Labour is necessary, to make intervals between his pleasures; his body has occasion for exercise, to co-order him with the beings who surround him; his heart must have desires; trouble alone can give him the right relish of his welfare; it is this which puts in the shadows, this which furnishes the true perspective to the picture of human life. By an irrevocable law of his destiny, man is obliged to be discontented with his present condition; to make efforts to change it; to reciprocally envy that felicity which no individual enjoys perfectly. Thus the poor man envies the opulence of his richer neighbour, although this is frequently more unhappy than his needy maligner; thus the rich man views with pain the advantages of a poverty, which he sees active, healthy, and frequently jocund, even in the bosom of penury.

If man was perfectly contented, there would no longer be any activity in the world; it is necessary that he should desire; it is requisite that he should act; it is incumbent he should labour, in order that he may be happy: such is the course of nature of which the life consists in action. Human societies can only subsist, by the continual exchange of those things in which man places his happiness. The poor man is obliged to desire, he is necessitated to labour, that he may procure what he knows is requisite to the preservation of his existence; the primary wants given to him by nature, are to nourish himself, clothe himself, lodge himself, and propagate his species; has he satisfied these? He is quickly obliged to create others entirely new; or rather, his imagination only refines upon the first; he seeks to diversify them; he is willing to give them fresh zest; arrived at opulence, when he has run over the whole circle of wants, when he has completely exhausted their combinations, he falls into disgust. Dispensed from labour, his body amasses humours; destitute of desires, his heart feels a languor; deprived of activity, he is obliged to participate his riches, with beings more active, more laborious than himself: these, following their own peculiar interests, take upon themselves the task of labouring for his advantage; of procuring for him means to satisfy his want; of ministering to his caprices, in order to remove the languor that oppresses him. It is thus the great, the rich excite the energies, give play to the activity, rouse the faculties, spur on the industry of the indigent; these labour to their own peculiar welfare by working for others: thus the desire of ameliorating his condition, renders man necessary to his fellow man; thus wants, always regenerating, never satisfied, are the principles of life,—the soul of activity,—the source of health,—the basis of society. If each individual was competent to the supply of his own exigencies, there would be no occasion for him to congregate in society; but it is his wants, his desires, his whims, that place him in a state of dependence on others: these are the causes that each individual, in order to further his own peculiar interest, is obliged to be useful to those, who have the capability of procuring for him the objects which he himself has not. A nation is nothing more than the union of a great number of individuals, connected with each other by the reciprocity of their wants; by their mutual desire of pleasure.

The most happy man is he who has the fewest wants, and who has the most numerous means of satisfying them. The man who would be truly rich, has no need to increase his fortune, it suffices he should diminish his wants.

In the individuals of the human species, as well as in political society, the progression of wants, is a thing absolutely necessary; it is founded upon the essence of man, it is requisite that the natural wants once satisfied, should be replaced by those which he calls *Imaginary, or wants of the Fancy:* these become as necessary to his happiness as the first. Custom, which permits the native American to go quite naked, obliges the more civilized inhabitant of Europe to clothe himself; the poor man contents himself with very simple attire, which equally serve him for winter and for summer, for autumn and for spring; the rich man desires to have garments suitable to each mutation of these seasons; he would experience pain if he had not the convenience of changing his raiment with every variation of his climate; he would be wretched if he was obliged to wear the same habiliments in the heat of summer, which he uses in the winter; in short, he would be unhappy if the expense and variety of his costume did not display to the surrounding multitude his opulence, mark his rank, announce his superiority. It is thus habit multiplies, the wants of the wealthy; it is thus that vanity itself becomes a want which sets a thousand hands in, motion, a thousand heads to work, who are all eager to gratify its cravings; in short, this very vanity procures for the necessitous man, the means of subsisting at the expense of his opulent neighbours He who is accustomed to pomp, who is used to ostentatious splendour, whose habits are luxurious, whenever he is deprived of these insignia of opulence, to which he has attached the idea of happiness, finds himself just as unhappy as the needy wretch who has not wherewith to cover his nakedness. The civilized nations of the present day were in their origin savages composed of erratic tribes,—mere wanderers who were occupied with war; employed in, the chace; painfully obliged to seek precarious subsistence by hunting in those woods which the industry of their successors has cleared; which their labour has covered with yellow waving ears of nutritious corn; in time they have become stationary: they first applied themselves to Agriculture, afterwards to commerce: by degrees they have refined on their primitive wants, extended their sphere of action, given birth to a thousand new wants, imagined a thousand new means to satisfy them; this is the natural course, the necessary progression, the regular march of active beings, who cannot live without feeling; who to be happy, must of necessity diversify their sensations. In proportion as man's wants multiply the means to satisfy them becomes more difficult, he is obliged to depend on a greater number of his fellow creatures; his interest obliges him to rouse their activity; to engage them to concur with his views; consequently he is obliged to procure for them those objects by which they can be excited; he is under the necessity of contenting their desires, which increase like his own, by the very food that satisfies them. The savage needs only put forth his hand to gather the fruit that offers itself spontaneously to his reach: this he finds sufficient for his nourishment. The opulent citizen of a flourishing society is obliged to set innumerable hands to work to produce the sumptuous repast; the four quarters of the globe are ransacked to procure the far-fetched viands become necessary to revive his languid appetite; the merchant, the sailor, the mechanic, leave nothing unattempted to flatter his inordinate vanity. From this it will appear, that in the same proportion the wants of man are multiplied, he is obliged to augment the means to satisfy them. Riches are nothing more than the measure of a convention, by the assistance of which man is enabled to make a great number of his fellows concur in the gratification of his desires; by which he is capacitated to invite them, for their own peculiar interests, to contribute to his pleasures. What, in fact, does the rich man do, except announce to the needy, that he can furnish him with the means of subsistence if he consents to lend himself to his will? What does the man in power, except shew to others, that he is in a state to supply the requisites to render them happy? Sovereigns, nobles, men of wealth, appear to be happy, only because they possess the ability, are masters of the motives sufficient to determine a great number of individuals to occupy themselves with their respective felicity.

The more things are considered the more man will be convinced that his false opinion are the true source of his misery; the clearer it will appear to him that happiness is so rare, only because he attaches it to objects either indifferent or useless to his welfare; which, when enjoyed, convert themselves into real evils; which afflict him; which become the cause of his misfortune.

Riches are indifferent in themselves, it is only by their application, by the purposes they compass, that they either become objects of utility to man, or are rendered prejudicial to his welfare.

Money, useless to the savage who understands not its value, is amassed by the miser, for fear it should be employed uselessly; lest it should be squandered by the prodigal; or dissipated by the voluptuary; who make no other use of it than to purchase infirmities; to buy regret.

Pleasures are nothing for the man who is incapable of feeling them; they become real evils when they are too freely indulged, when they are destructive to his health,— when they derange the economy of his machine,—when they entail diseases on himself and on his posterity,— when they make him neglect his duties,—when they render him despicable in the eyes of others.

Power is nothing in itself, it is useless to man if he does not avail himself of it to promote his own peculiar felicity, by augmenting the happiness of his species; it becomes fatal to him as soon as he abuses it; it becomes odious whenever he employs it to render others miserable; it is always the cause of his own misery whenever he stretches it beyond the due bounds prescribed by nature.

For want of being enlightened on his true interest, the man who enjoys all the means of rendering himself completely happy, scarcely ever discovers the secret of making those means truly subservient to his own peculiar felicity: the art of enjoying, is that which of all others is least understood; man should learn this art before he begins to desire; the earth is covered with individuals who only occupy themselves with the care of procuring the means without ever being acquainted with the end. All the world desire fortune, solicit power, seek after pleasure, yet very few, indeed, are those whom objects render truly happy.

It is quite natural in man, it is extremely reasonable, it is absolutely necessary, to desire those things which can contribute to augment the sum of his felicity. *Pleasure, riches, power,* are objects worthy his ambition, deserving his most strenuous efforts, when he has learned how to employ them; when he has acquired the faculty of making them render his existence really more agreeable. It is impossible to censure him who desires them, to despise him who commands them, but when to obtain them he employs odious means; or when after he has obtained them he makes a pernicious use of them, injurious to himself, prejudicial to others; let him wish for power, let him seek after grandeur, let him be ambitious of reputation, when he can shew just pretensions to them; when he can obtain them, without making the purchase at the expence of his own repose, or that of the beings with whom he lives: let him desire riches, when he knows how to make a use of them that is truly advantageous for himself, really beneficial for others; but never let him employ those means to procure them of which he may be ashamed; with which he may be obliged to reproach himself; which may draw upon him the hatred of his associates; or which may render him obnoxious to the castigation of society: let him always recollect, that his solid happiness should rest its foundations upon its own esteem,—upon the advantages he procures for others; above all, never let him for a moment forget, that of all the objects to which his ambition may point, the most impracticable for a being who lives in society, is that of *attempting to render himself exclusively happy.*

Essay on the Secret of Abounding Happiness[5]

Even though most people will admit that selfishness is the cause of all the unhappiness in the world, they fall under the soul-destroying delusion that it is somebody else's selfishness, and not their own.

When you are willing to admit that all your unhappiness is the result of your own selfishness you will not be far from the gates of Paradise; but so long as you are convinced that it is the selfishness of others that is robbing you of joy, so long will you

---

[5] Based on the work of James Allen, in *From Poverty to Power; or, the Realization of Prosperity and Peace*, 1901

remain a prisoner in your self-created purgatory.

Happiness is that inward state of perfect satisfaction which is joy and peace, and from which all desire is eliminated. The satisfaction which results from gratified desire is brief and illusionary, and is always followed by an increased demand for gratification.

Desire is as insatiable as the ocean, and clamors louder and louder as its demands are attended to.

It claims ever-increasing service from its deluded devotees, until at last they are struck down with physical or mental anguish, and are hurled into the purifying fires of suffering. Desire is the region of hell, and all torments are centered there.

The giving up of desire is the realization of heaven, and all delights await the pilgrim there.

I sent my soul through the invisible,
Some letter of that after life to spell,
And by-and-by my soul returned to me,
And whispered, I myself am heaven and hell"

Heaven and hell are inward states. Sink into self and all its gratifications, and you sink into hell; rise above self into that state of consciousness which is the utter denial and forgetfulness of self, and you enter heaven.

Self is blind, without judgment, not possessed of true knowledge, and always leads to suffering. Correct perception, unbiased judgment, and true knowledge belong only to the divine state, and only in so far as you realize this divine consciousness can you know what real happiness is.

So long as you persist in selfishly seeking for your own personal happiness, so long will happiness elude you, and you will be sowing the seeds of wretchedness.

In so far as you succeed in losing yourself in the service of others, in that measure will happiness come to you, and you will reap a harvest of bliss.

It is in loving, not in being loved,
The heart is blessed;
It is in giving, not in seeking gifts,
We find our quest.
Whatever be thy longing or thy need,
That do thou give;
So shall thy soul be fed, and thou indeed
Shalt truly live.

Cling to self, and you cling to sorrow, relinquish self, and you enter into peace. To seek selfishly is not only to lose happiness, but even that which we believe to be the source of happiness.

See how the glutton is continually looking about for a new delicacy wherewith to stimulate his deadened appetite; and how, bloated, burdened, and diseased, scarcely any food at last is eaten with pleasure.

Whereas, he who has mastered his appetite, and not only does not seek, but never thinks of gustatory pleasure, finds delight in the most frugal meal. The angel-form of happiness, which men, looking through the eyes of self, imagine they see in gratified desire, when clasped is always found to be the skeleton of misery. Truly,

"He that seeketh his life shall lose it, and he that loseth his life shall find it."

Abiding happiness will come to you when, ceasing to selfishly cling, you are willing to give up. When you are willing to lose, unreservedly, that impermanent thing which is so dear to you, and which, whether you cling to it or not, will one day be snatched from you, then you will find that that which seemed to you like a painful loss, turns out to be a supreme gain.

To give up in order to gain, than this there is no greater delusion, nor no more prolific source of misery; but to be willing to yield up and to suffer loss, this is indeed the Way of Life.

How is it possible to find real happiness by centering ourselves in those things which, by their very nature, must pass away? Abiding and real happiness can only be found by centering ourselves in that which is permanent.

Rise, therefore, above the clinging to and the craving for impermanent things, and you will then enter into a consciousness of the Eternal, and as, rising above self, and by growing more and more into the spirit of purity, self-sacrifice and universal Love, you become centered in that consciousness, you will realize that happiness which has no reaction, and which can never be taken from you.

The heart that has reached utter self-forgetfulness in its love for others has not only become possessed of the highest happiness but has entered into immortality, for it has realized the Divine.

Look back upon your life, and you will find that the moments of supremest happiness were those in which you uttered some word, or performed some act, of compassion or self-denying love. Spiritually, happiness and harmony are, synonymous.

Harmony is one phase of the Great Law whose spiritual expression is love. All selfishness is discord, and to be selfish is to be out of harmony with the Divine order.

As we realize that all-embracing love which is the negation of self, we put ourselves in harmony with the divine music, the universal song, and that ineffable melody which is true happiness becomes our own.

Men and women are rushing hither and thither in the blind search for happiness, and cannot find it; nor ever will until they recognize that happiness is already within them and round about them, filling the universe, and that they, in their selfish searching are shutting themselves out from it.

I followed happiness to make her mine, Past towering oak and swinging ivy vine. She fled, I chased, o'er slanting hill and dale, O'er fields and meadows, in the purpling vale; Pursuing rapidly o'er dashing stream.

I scaled the dizzy cliffs where eagles scream; I traversed swiftly every land and

M. But always happiness eluded me. Exhausted, fainting, I pursued no more, But sank to rest upon a barren shore.

One came and asked for food, and one for alms I placed the bread and gold in bony palms.

One came for sympathy, and one for rest; I shared with every needy one my best; When, Io! sweet Happiness, with form divine, Stood by me, whispering softly, 'I am thine'.

These beautiful lines of Burleigh's express the secret of all abounding happiness. Sacrifice the personal and transient, and you rise at once into the impersonal and permanent.

Give up that narrow cramped self that seeks to render all things subservient to its own petty interests, and you will enter into the company of the angels, into the very heart and essence of universal Love.

Forget yourself entirely in the sorrows of others and in ministering to others, and divine happiness will emancipate you from all sorrow and suffering.

"Taking the first step with a good thought, the second with a good word, and the third with a good deed, I entered Paradise." And you also may enter into Paradise by pursuing the same course. It is not beyond, it is here. It is realized only by the unselfish.

It is known in its fullness only to the pure in heart. If you have not realized this unbounded happiness you may begin to actualize it by ever holding before you the lofty ideal of unselfish love, and aspiring towards it.

Aspiration or prayer is desire turned upward. It is the soul turning toward its Divine source, where alone permanent satisfaction can be found. By aspiration the destructive forces of desire are transmuted into divine and all-preserving energy.

To aspire is to make an effort to shake off the trammels of desire; it is the prodigal made wise by loneliness and suffering, returning to his Father's Mansion.

As you rise above the sordid self; as you break, one after another, the chains that bind you, will you realize the joy of giving, as distinguished from the misery of grasping - giving of your substance; giving of your intellect; giving of the love and light that is growing within you.

You will then understand that it is indeed "more blessed to give than to receive." But the giving must be of the heart without any taint of self, without desire for reward. The gift of pure love is always attended with bliss. If, after you have given, you are wounded because you are not thanked or flattered, or your name put in the paper, know then that your gift was prompted by vanity and not by love, and you were merely giving in order to get; were not really giving, but grasping.

Lose yourself in the welfare of others; forget yourself in all that you do; this is the secret of abounding happiness.

Ever be on the watch to guard against selfishness, and learn faithfully the divine lessons of inward sacrifice; so shall you climb the highest heights of happiness, and shall remain in the neverclouded sunshine of universal joy, clothed in the shining garment of immortality.

Are you searching for the happiness that does not fade away?

Are you looking for the joy that lives, and leaves no grievous day?

Are you panting for the waterbrooks of Love, and Life, and Peace?

Then let all dark desires depart, and selfish seeking cease.

Are you ling'ring in the paths of pain, grief-haunted, stricken sore?

Are you wand'ring in the ways that wound your weary feet the more?

Are you sighing for the Resting-Place where tears and sorrows cease?

Then sacrifice your selfish heart and find the Heart of Peace.

Road to Happiness[6]

Happiness is the greatest paradox in Nature. It can grow in any soil, live under any conditions. It defies environment. It comes from within; it is the revelation of the depths of the inner life as light and heat proclaim the sun from which they radiate. Happiness consists not of having, but of being; not of possessing, but of enjoying. It is the warm glow of a heart at peace with itself. A martyr at the stake may have happiness that a king on his throne might envy. Man is the creator of his own happiness; it is the aroma of a life lived in harmony with high ideals. For what a man has, he may be dependent on others; what

---

[6] Based on the work of William George Jordan.

he is, rests with him alone. What he obtains in life is but acquisition; what he attains, is growth. Happiness is the soul's joy in the possession of the intangible. Absolute, perfect, continuous happiness in life, is impossible for the human. It would mean the consummation of attainments, the individual consciousness of a perfectly fulfilled destiny. Happiness is paradoxic because it may coexist with trial, sorrow and poverty. It is the gladness of the heart,--rising superior to all conditions.

Happiness has a number of under-studies,--gratification, satisfaction, content, and pleasure,--clever imitators that simulate its appearance rather than emulate its method. Gratification is a harmony between our desires and our possessions. It is ever incomplete, it is the thankful acceptance of part. It is a mental pleasure in the quality of what one receives, an unsatisfiedness as to the quantity. It may be an element in happiness, but, in itself,--it is not happiness.

Satisfaction is perfect identity of our desires and our possessions. It exists only so long as this perfect union and unity can be preserved. But every realized ideal gives birth to new ideals, every step in advance reveals large domains of the unattained; every feeding stimulates new appetites,-- then the desires and possessions are no longer identical, no longer equal; new cravings call forth new activities, the equipoise is destroyed, and dissatisfaction reenters. Man might possess everything tangible in the world and yet not be happy, for happiness is the satisfying of the soul, not of the mind or the body. Dissatisfaction, in its highest sense, is the keynote of all advance, the evidence of new aspirations, the guarantee of the progressive revelation of new possibilities.

Content is a greatly overrated virtue. It is a kind of diluted despair; it is the feeling with which we continue to accept substitutes, without striving for the realities. Content makes the trained individual swallow vinegar and try to smack his lips as if it were wine. Content enables one to warm his hands at the fire of a past joy that exists only in memory. Content is a mental and moral chloroform that deadens the activities of the individual to rise to higher planes of life and growth. Man should never be contented with anything less than the best efforts of his nature can possibly secure for him. Content makes the world more comfortable for the individual, but it is the death-knell of progress. Man should be content with each step of progress merely as a station, discontented with it as a destination; contented with it as a step; discontented with it as a finality. There are times when a man should be content with what he has, but never with what he is.

But content is not happiness; neither is pleasure. Pleasure is temporary, happiness is continuous; pleasure is a note, happiness is a symphony; pleasure may exist when conscience utters protests; happiness,-- never. Pleasure may have its dregs and its lees; but none can be found in the cup of happiness.

Man is the only animal that can be really happy. To the rest of the creation belong only weak imitations of the understudies. Happiness represents a peaceful attunement of a life with a standard of living. It can never be made by the individual, by himself, for himself. It is one of the incidental by-products of an unselfish life. No man can make his own happiness the one object of his life and attain it, any more than he can jump on the far end of his shadow. If you would hit the bull's-eye of happiness on the target of life, aim above it. Place other things higher than your own happiness and it will surely come to you. You can buy pleasure, you can acquire content, you can become satisfied,--but Nature never put real happiness on the bargain-counter. It is the undetachable accompaniment of true living. It is calm and peaceful; it never lives in an atmosphere of worry or of hopeless struggle.

The basis of happiness is the love of something outside self. Search every instance of happiness in the world, and you will find, when all the incidental features are eliminated, there is always the constant, unchangeable element of love,--love of parent for child; love of man and woman for each other; love of humanity in some form, or a great life work into which the individual throws all his energies.

Happiness is the voice of optimism, of faith, of simple, steadfast love. No cynic or pessimist can be really happy. A cynic is a man who is morally near-sighted,--and brags about it. He sees the evil in his own heart, and thinks he sees the world. He lets a mote in his eye eclipse the sun. An incurable cynic is an individual who should long for death,--for life cannot bring him happiness, death might. The keynote of Bismarck's lack of happiness was his profound distrust of human nature.

There is a royal road to happiness; it lies in Consecration, Concentration, Conquest and Conscience.

Consecration is dedicating the individual life to the service of others, to some noble mission, to realizing some unselfish ideal. Life is not something to be lived through; it is something to be lived up to. It is a privilege, not a penal servitude of so many decades on earth. Consecration places the object of life above the mere acquisition of money, as a finality. The man who is unselfish, kind, loving, tender, helpful, ready to lighten the burden of those around him, to hearten the struggling ones, to forget himself sometimes in remembering others,--is on the right road to happiness. Consecration is ever active, bold and aggressive, fearing naught but possible disloyalty to high ideals.

Concentration makes the individual life simpler and deeper. It cuts away the shams and pretences of modern living and limits life to its truest essentials. Worry, fear, useless regret,--all the great wastes that sap mental, moral or physical energy must be sacrificed, or the individual needlessly destroys half the possibilities of living. A great purpose in life, something that unifies the strands and threads of each day's thinking, something that takes the sting from the petty trials, sorrows, sufferings and blunders of life, is a great aid to Concentration. Soldiers in battle may forget their wounds, or even be unconscious of them, in the inspiration of battling for what they believe is right. Concentration dignifies an humble life; it makes a great life,-- sublime. In morals it is a short-cut to simplicity. It leads to right for right's sake, without thought of policy or of reward. It brings calm and rest to the individual,--a serenity that is but the sunlight of happiness.

Conquest is the overcoming of an evil habit, the rising superior to opposition and attack, the spiritual exaltation that comes from resisting the invasion of the grovelling material side of life. Sometimes when you are worn and weak with the struggle; when it seems that justice is a dream, that honesty and loyalty and truth count for nothing, that the devil is the only good paymaster; when hope grows dim and flickers, then is the time when you must tower in the great sublime faith that Right must prevail, then must you throttle these imps of doubt and despair, you must master yourself to master the world around you. This is Conquest; this is what counts. Even a log can float with the current, it takes a man to fight sturdily against an opposing tide that would sweep his craft out of its course. When the jealousies, the petty intrigues and the meannesses and the misunderstandings in life assail you,--rise above them. Be like a lighthouse that illumines and beautifies the snarling, swashing waves of the storm that threaten it, that seek to undermine it and seek to wash over it. This is Conquest.

When the chance to win fame, wealth, success or the attainment of your heart's desire, by sacrifice of honor or principle, comes to you and it does not affect you long enough even to seem a temptation, you have been the victor. That too is Conquest. And Conquest is part of the royal road to Happiness.

Conscience, as the mentor, the guide and compass of every act, leads ever to Happiness. When the individual can stay alone with his conscience and get its approval, without using force or specious logic, then he begins to know what real Happiness is. But the individual must be careful that he is not appealing to a conscience perverted or deadened by the wrongdoing and subsequent deafness of its owner. The man who is honestly seeking to live his life in Consecration, Concentration and Conquest, living from day to day as best he can, by the light he has, may rely explicitly on his Conscience. He can shut his ears to "what the world says" and find in the approval of his own conscience the highest earthly tribune,--the voice of the Infinite communing with the Individual.

Unhappiness is the hunger to get; Happiness is the hunger to give. True happiness must ever have the tinge of sorrow outlived, the sense of pain softened by the mellowing years, the chastening of loss that in the wondrous mystery of time transmutes our suffering into love and sympathy with others.

If the individual should set out for a single day to give Happiness, to make life happier, brighter and sweeter, not for himself, but for others, he would find a wondrous revelation of what Happiness really is. The greatest of the world's heroes could not by any series of acts of heroism do as much real good as any individual living his whole life in seeking, from day to day, to make others happy.

Each day there should be fresh resolution, new strength, and renewed enthusiasm. "Just for Today" might be the daily motto of thousands of societies throughout the country, composed of members bound together to make the world better through constant simple acts of kindness, constant deeds of sweetness and love. And Happiness would come to them, in its highest and best form, not because they would seek to absorb it, but, because they seek to radiate it.

*

This reflection on the happiness will have reached its goal, if it leads the reader to think that man, by exercising his faculties, can soften his troubles, multiply his pleasures; and therefore, help him to make the choice to be happy regardless of his socio-economic conditions.